The Voyage of Odysseus

Tales from the Odyssey

Written by I. M. Richardson
Illustrated by Hal Frenck

Troll Associates

Library of Congress Cataloging in Publication Data

Richardson, I. M.
    The voyage of Odysseus.

    (Tales from the Odyssey / adapted by I. M. Richardson;
bk. 1)
      Summary: While Odysseus is being held by Calypso on
an island, Telemachos searches for his father and
Penelope is besieged with suitors.
     [1. Mythology, Greek] I. Frenck, Hal, ill.
II. Homer. Odyssey. III. Title. IV. Series:
Richardson, I. M. Tales from the Odyssey; bk. 1.
PZ8.1.R396Tal 1984 bk. 1 292'.13s [292'.13] 83-14235
ISBN 0-8167-0005-2 (lib. bdg.)
ISBN 0-8167-0006-0 (pbk.)

Nearly ten years had passed since the fall of Troy. The victors of the long Trojan War had returned to their homes and families in Greece. But Odysseus, King of the Greek island called Ithaca, had not yet returned. He had suffered one misfortune after another. He had lost his ships and all of his men. Now he was being held prisoner on an island in the sea.

High above, on Mount Olympus, the gods were holding a meeting. All were present except Poseidon, god of the ocean. Zeus, the chief god, spoke first. "Poseidon is still angry with Odysseus," he said. "But instead of killing him, he has kept him from returning to his beloved homeland."

Then Athena, goddess of wisdom, said, "Now Poseidon has sent Odysseus to Calypso's island. Calypso holds the poor man there and keeps him from returning home. Let us send a message to her, ordering her to set him free. Meanwhile, I will go to Ithaca and look in on the troubled house of Odysseus."

Dozens of rude young noblemen had made themselves at home in the house of Odysseus. They sought the hand of Penelope, the faithful wife of the absent king. Telemachos, the son of Odysseus, wished his father would return and throw them all out. Suddenly, he saw a stranger at the door. It was really Athena, disguised as a mortal.

Athena said, "My name is Mentes, and I have come to visit with my old friend, Odysseus. Unfortunately, I see that the gods have delayed his return. Nonetheless, I tell you that he will be home soon. Now you must listen closely to the advice I will give you, and you must do exactly as I say."

The next day, Telemachos called together the people of Ithaca. An old prophet stood up and said, "Long ago, I prophesied that Odysseus would have many troubles and return unrecognized by everyone. Now I say that he will return soon and destroy the unwelcome suitors in his house." But someone else called out, "Odysseus is dead! Let Penelope choose a new husband!"

Then, following the advice he had received from Athena, Telemachos said, "Who will lend me a fast ship and twenty men? I must go to Sparta and back, seeking news of my father. If I learn that he is dead, my mother will marry another husband." The suitors laughed at him, certain that he would never make such a voyage.

After the meeting had ended, the suitors went back to the house of Odysseus to eat and drink. Meanwhile, with Athena's help, Telemachos borrowed a ship and gathered a crew together. He told his housekeeper to prepare supplies for a voyage. "But tell no one," he said.

That night, the supplies were secretly taken to the harbor and loaded on board the ship. Then Telemachos went aboard and ordered the crew to cast off the lines and put out to sea. When they had rowed far enough from the shore to catch an evening breeze, they hoisted the sails and disappeared into the night.

The next day, they stopped at the home of an old and talkative king named Nestor. Nestor had fought next to Odysseus in the Trojan War. When he heard why Telemachos had come, Nestor rambled on and on, reliving the sacking of Troy. But he had no new information about Odysseus. "My advice is to go to Sparta and speak with King Menelaos," he said. "Perhaps he can help you."

When Telemachos finally reached Sparta, a wedding feast was in progress. King Menelaos welcomed him and asked him to join in the celebration. He sat down next to Menelaos' beautiful wife. Her name was Helen, and it was she for whom the Trojan War had been fought. She knew at once that Telemachos was the son of Odysseus.

Telemachos explained that he had come in search of news about his father. Then his host replied, "I can only tell you what I learned from the Old Man of the Sea—that servant of Poseidon who knows every corner of the vast ocean. He told me that he saw Odysseus."

"Where?" asked Telemachos. And Menelaos replied, "The Old Man of the Sea told me that he saw Odysseus on an island in the middle of the sea. He said that Calypso, the daughter of Atlas, holds him as a captive there." Then Telemachos thanked his host and said, "Knowing that my father is alive will give me the strength to carry on until he returns home."

Meanwhile, the suitors discovered that Telemachos had left Ithaca. They feared that he might cause trouble for them when he returned. They knew that he would have to pass through a narrow strait on his way home. So they sailed out and anchored there, hoping to ambush him.

Their scheme was overheard by a faithful servant, who went at once to Penelope with the news. "I have already lost my husband," cried Penelope. "Must I now lose my son as well?" But that night, Athena appeared to the queen in a dream and told her that Telemachos would return to her safely.

When Athena returned to Mount Olympus, Zeus sent Hermes, the messenger god, down to Calypso's island. Hermes found Calypso in her cave and said, "Zeus commands you to release your prisoner." Calypso was not pleased, for she had fallen in love with Odysseus, but she could not refuse a command from Zeus.

As soon as Hermes had gone, Calypso went to her captive. "Cheer up, Odysseus! You are free to go. All you have to do is build a raft. Then you can sail home to Ithaca," she told him. "A raft?" questioned the wary Odysseus. "This sounds like one of your tricks. It is difficult enough to cross the sea in a sturdy ship. I could never do it on a raft!"

But Calypso assured him that it was not a trick. Then she took him to a grove of trees and gave him an ax. He began to cut down trees, and trim them, and shape them. Then Calypso brought him other tools, and he carefully fitted the logs together and locked them in place with wooden pegs.

After four days of labor, he had built a sturdy raft. It had a strong mast and a massive steering oar. When provisions for a long journey had been loaded aboard, Odysseus pushed the raft out into deep water. Then the wind filled the sail, and he set his course for home.

For seventeen days, Odysseus sailed over the open sea. Finally, on the eighteenth day, he spotted an island in the distance. But at the same time, Poseidon, the angry god of the ocean, spotted Odysseus. He called up a terrible storm, with winds that howled and whipped the water into great waves. Odysseus was swept overboard into the sea.

He managed to climb back onto the raft but was nearly swept off again and again. Then a lovely sea goddess appeared and called out, "Take this veil and dive into the sea. When you reach shore, toss it back to me." Odysseus looked at the flimsy veil and at the angry waves. Was this the trick of a vengeful god?

He decided to stay with his raft as long as it was still afloat. Finally the mast snapped, and the vessel was torn apart. Odysseus leaped into the churning sea. As he neared the coast, he saw that he would be smashed against the jagged rocks if he tried to go ashore there.

He swam along until he came to a river that rushed headlong into the sea. The river god took pity on him and slowed the river's current. Odysseus swam into the mouth of the river, where he saw a sandy beach. Exhausted, he crawled up on shore, then turned and threw the veil back into the water. Moments later, he was asleep in the bushes beneath two olive trees.

In the morning, he was awakened by the happy sounds of several maidens, who had come to the river to wash some clothes. When he approached, they ran away. Only one remained. She was a princess whose mother and father ruled the island. She gave Odysseus fresh clothing and told him how he might win the favor of her parents, Queen Arete and King Alcinous.

That night, Odysseus went to the palace of the king and queen. Athena hid him in a heavy mist, so no one saw him approach the great mansion. No one saw him pass through the doorway or down the halls. And no one saw him as he made his way past the lords and ladies who were at the banquet with the king and queen.

When the mist cleared, Odysseus was kneeling in front of
the queen. "Queen Arete," he said, "take pity on me, for I
have been washed ashore on your island. Send me home to
my native land." He was offered a seat of honor at the table.
Delicious foods were set before him, and he ate heartily.

When the other guests had departed, the queen turned to Odysseus and said, "If you were washed up on our shores, then who gave you the fresh clothing you are wearing?" In answer, Odysseus told her everything that had happened since he had left Calypso's island. Then King Alcinous said, "Tomorrow, we shall launch a ship to take you home."

The next morning, a new ship was moored in the deep water of the harbor. Fifty-two of the best oarsmen on the island were selected for its crew. King Alcinous stood in the meeting square with Odysseus and announced, "This stranger has come to us and asked for help in reaching his distant home. Of course, we shall grant his request, for we are always ready to help wayward travelers."

Then everyone went to the king's mansion for sports and
games. There were foot races and wrestling matches. There
was a discus throw. Odysseus was challenged to try his
luck, and his throw was farther than anyone else's. Finally
the sun began to set, and they all went into the house for a
farewell dinner for their guest.

After he had eaten, Odysseus told everyone about the adventures with which his homeward voyage had been filled. And as he told of his odyssey, he thought of his home—and he smiled. For he knew that tomorrow his journey would finally come to an end. At last, he would be home again in Ithaca.